All things relate

All things relate

*Babs, with love
Angela Greenhill
27.1.96*

Poems by
ANGELA GREENHILL

Illustrations by MARY ALLAN & others

London 1995

First published in 1995
Copyright © Angela Greenhill
All rights reserved

ISBN 1 900496 11 9

Designed, produced and published for the author
by Kitzinger, 17 Willow St, London EC2A 4QH

Printed and bound by Smith Settle, Otley

For Denis

Contents

Acknowledgements 9
Foreword *by Auberon Waugh* 11
Persephone Reborn 15
Thyme in Sabratha 17
And the Dogs Ate Jezebel 19
Seesaw Proposal 21
Soldier's Child 22
The Patriots 23
La Vie en Rose 25
Dear John 26
First Love 27
Broken Idol 28
The Cracked Vase 29
Red Roses for Sam 30
Removal 31
Fresh 32
Feelings 33
Hope 34
Night Horrors 35
The Happy Hour 37
'Wer spricht von Siegen?' 38
Rendezvous 41
Massed Choirs in Westminster Abbey, 1937 42
Going Home 43
Fairy Godmother 44
Cinders 45
Early Words 46
The Silver Pig 47
Small Survivor 48
First Born 49
Plus ça Change 50
To a china john 51
Silver Jubilee 1977 52
Rosaceous 53
Poh Lin 54

The French Children 55
Low Days 56
Giddy Nights 57
The Prudent Gardener 58
Apples of Gold 59
Little Werrar Wood 61
December Legacy 63
Foursquare 65

Illustrations 67

Notes 69

Acknowledgements

Firstly, I should like to thank Auberon Waugh and the *Literary Review* for kind encouragement to a rather late starter.

I am also very grateful to Mary Allan who has made many of the charming illustrations for this book.

Fernand and Helga Auberjonois contributed invaluable help and advice, as did Diana and Richard Holderness. I should also like to thank Tony Kitzinger for his design of the book.

Lastly and especially I thank my husband who in everything has never wavered in his support.

Angela Greenhill
London, 1995

Foreword

by Auberon Waugh

I first made the acquaintance of Angela Greenhill's poetry as a judge for the monthly Grand Poetry Competition set by my magazine, the *Literary Review*, for the best lines in the formal tradition – that is to say, which rhymes, scans and makes sense – on a different set subject every month.

We are often mocked, by the modernists, for publishing what they call 'Granny Poems', and I was delighted to learn, when Angela won 1994's Grand Prize for the best poem of the year, that she is a grandmother. Her verse has a lightness of touch and a sense of irony which go very well with the sadder themes of loss and bereavement. I do not think that such a combination would be available to younger poets who had not lived through the last war.

At any rate, I am proud to have been a member of the panel which recognised her talent and proud also that so many of the excellent poems she wrote for the *Literary Review* have found a more permanent home in this delightful book. It deserves to sell in its tens of thousands, and I hope it does.

All things relate

Persephone Reborn

For Aster

Persephone arose the other day
Not as a goddess but a girl at play,
Dressed in white net, a garland on her head
'I am the bride of Hades!' (so she said)
Laughing and blushing, all her long fair hair
Falling like April sunshine everywhere.
Something she lacked perhaps of Attic grace
But yet the spring itself was in her face
The very spring in all its loveliness.
Hard to believe it was just fancy dress.

And for a moment I was lost in time
Back in another land, another clime,
Another nymph rose radiant from the earth,
An older spring reblossomed into birth,
Persephone returned with flower-crowned head
Triumphant from the kingdom of the dead.

Thyme in Sabratha

For Robin

This poem won't get itself written
    Tied up in a tangle of rhyme
Yet I remember Sabratha
    Whenever I season with thyme

For it grows in those Roman ruins
    Close to the ancient sea,
And I remember Sabratha
    Because you were there with me.

Too simple? A herb is simple
    And so is the cry of the heart.
You that were part of my being
    Are now a being apart.

Are you cold out there in the darkness?
    Or incandescent, refined
Into a loving spirit
    Part of the cosmic mind?

Wherever you are I shall find you
    Beyond these mortal bars
On that uncharted journey
    Out to the furthest stars,

So here's rosemary for remembrance,
    Rue for the herb of grace
And traveller's joy for my darling
    Gone to another place.

And the Dogs Ate Jezebel

Up North, where the wind blew sharp as a whistle
And the gulls screamed blue murder down the grey Clyde,
Lived an old lady as tough as a thistle
With her Bible as mentor, companion and guide.

And she told bedtime stories of real blood and thunder
To two wide-eyed children agog in the dark:
The Death of Goliath, the Sea Cleft Asunder,
Jael and her Hammer, Noah and his Ark,

Elijah whirled up in a great fiery chariot,
Absalom hung by his hair from a tree
And that wicked old sinner Judas Iscariot
Rotted in hell for eternity.

King David when old became rather naughty
And took a young wife to warm his cold feet,
Queen Vashti lost out for being too haughty,
And the dogs ate Jezebel in the street!

I'm sure her back hurt her, yet bent almost double
Nightly she climbed to our bedroom above,
For we must have our story whatever the trouble.
It is a light burden, the labour of love.

When I married in wartime, afar in a hot land,
Came a cable to Cairo, a voice from the past,
'A good wife's above rubies!' wired Granny-in-Scotland,
Loving, God-fearing and true to the last.

Should I stray from the way her ghost would remind me
That Someone is watching my wandering feet,
That the God of Elijah is there just behind me
And the dogs ate Jezebel in the street!

Seesaw Proposal

"Oh Alice, dear Alice, sweet Alice St. George
    With a name like a song and eyes like the sea
Now grave and now smiling, please say you will be
    My Alice for now and eternity.

Perched up there on high like a bird on a bough,
    Fresh as a rose in your pretty new dress,
You cannot come down until I seesaw up
    And I won't budge an inch until you answer 'Yes!'"

Of course she said 'Yes', what else could she do?
    Their first child was my mother. One might speculate
Where I should be now if she'd answered 'No'
    Where tossed and where dropped by the seesaw of Fate?

I'm glad she said 'Yes' for I like to belong
To that long-ago girl with a name like a song.

Soldier's Child

'BANG BANG goes my gun,
I'll shoot you all dead!'
'Be quiet, little son

The tale is not done.
There's a true one instead
BANG BANG went the gun

With a shot NOT in fun
And your Dad lay outspread
(Stay quiet, little son).

With no victory won,
But a hole in his head.
BANG BANG went the gun

That made his blood run.
Now they've put him to bed
(Stay quiet, little son).

With none near him, none.
He sleeps sound, so it's said
Where BANG BANG went the gun.

Deep, deep sleep the dead.'

The Patriots

War's a dead loss
And mocks Love on the Cross,
    None the less we will strive
By land and by sea
In the air if need be
    Against all men alive
Who would tread with iron heel
On our necks, make us kneel,
    Who would plot and connive
To steal what's our own,
The fields we have sown,
    The towns we made thrive;
Who would ravage the earth,
The land of our birth
    And of Liberty bright.
As the dead from the tomb,
As the babe from the womb,
    We will rise in our might,
Make no mistake,
All bonds we will break –
    We will *die* for our right
Or live to be free –
Brother, link arms with me,
    Together we fight.

La Vie en Rose

Give me the lime, the yew, the box
And cherry-pie that smells so sweet,
Heavy-scented summer stocks
Growing near a garden seat,
Rosemary, belovéd herb,
Pansies aping human faces,
Sunflowers dreaming they are clocks,
Daisies in forbidden places,
Lavender to dry on sheets,
Gypsy-like anemones
And every sweet the garden boasts
That I may pick them as I please
And give me roses, roses, roses,
Every kind of rose that grows,
Till I am buried deep in petals
And all the world is one vast rose.

Dear John

I meant to write a month ago
But could not find the words to say
What I should have let you know
Tomorrow is my wedding day.

We made no promise, swore no vow,
Never said we'd love no other,
Why then so hard to tell you now
That I am marrying another?

It never could have worked, we knew,
We came from worlds too far apart
And yet the steady liking grew
From eye to mind, from mind to heart.

Much can happen in a year,
Time and space can come between
Two who hold each other dear.
I sometimes think what might have been

Might have been, but never was.
In years to come we shall be glad
We left things unresolved, because
We kept unspoiled the dream we had.

How I adored your chiselled lips,
Your handsome head, your stalwart shape
But did not love your cycle clips
Much less that yellow oilskin cape!

First Love

After Flaischlen

'Always with roses in your hand I saw you,
Only so it seems I saw you stand
With laughing lips and roses in your hand,
Deep in your heart a secret song;
So once I thought all life after
Must be roses, sunshine and laughter
To the hidden music of a secret song.'

Only a faded rose now tells that story
Pressed in my book and, copied in your hand,
Those gentle lines that will forever stand
Deep in my heart; stilled is the secret song.
So short for you the life that followed after
Those happy days of roses and of laughter.
That hidden music was a bullet's song.

Now I alone recall that old enchantment,
That time of roses in a foreign land,
That bitter war we could not understand,
The happiness that did not linger long;
For sorrow took the place of carefree laughter,
The shape of things was otherwise thereafter
And life moved onwards to a harsher song.

Broken Idol

When I was young and tender-hearted
   There was one I loved as dearly
   As all the world beside, or nearly,
Until sad disillusion started

And I discovered day by day
   A truth that took some bitter learning,
   Though clear enough to the discerning,
That idols can have feet of clay

And uglier failings, past forgiving.
   Feet of clay have this demerit
   They trample down the loving spirit
To point of death. But life's for living

And we abjure because we must
Broken idols smashed to dust.

The Cracked Vase

Translation from 'Le Vase Brisé', Sully Prudhomme 1839–1901

The vase where this verbena's dying
Suffered the merest little knock,
A fan's light tap (no cause for crying),
No sound betrayed the secret shock.

Yet this slight wound, though only glancing,
Eats at the crystal day by day,
And by its stealthy sure advancing
Circles the fragile life away.

The water's drop by drop diminished,
The sap has spent itself in token.
None now can doubt that it is finished.
Do not touch it. It is broken.

Often so the hand we cherish
Will wound the heart in passing by.
Then of itself the heart will perish,
Its flower of love will wilt and die.

Daily deeper bites the throbbing
Small sharp wound that none can see
Save the heart, in secret sobbing.
It is broken. Let it be.

Red Roses for Sam

July in Paris, candlelight on silver,
Roses on the table, crimson and full-blown,
An American to dinner for a party in his honour,
Sam, as dear a colleague as any we had known.

Below our master windows lights shone on the river,
Bateaux mouches sped busily up and down the Seine,
All the guests were happy as they left by moonlight,
And Sam, we felt quite certain, would soon be back again.

I still can see those roses, each scented petal trembling
On the edge of falling, wanting to be free,
While through the open windows the water whispered softly
As the Seine pursued untroubled her sure way to the sea.

Friends like flowers are fragile although we hold them dear.
Sam had gone for ever; he died within the year.

Removal

For Marcella

They were packing up your life as I came by,
Your books, your pictures and your kindly ways,
Encasing the sum total of your days.
They were packing up your life as I came by.

Down in the courtyard stood the empty van
Filling up with boxes, one by one,
Your charming porcelain and your sense of fun.
Complete the packers' list? Of course I can!

All those lame dogs you hefted over stiles
Would fill a van or two; sad souls you comforted;
Old folk you cherished; hungry ones you fed;
And I could stuff a suitcase with your smiles.

Now you are gone, the keys turned in the locks,
I think of all the things I might have said.
Too late. There is no converse with the dead.
You and all your life are in a box.

I know all this. Why then my shocked surprise?
The van drives off into the vast unknown
And disappears. I stand there quite alone
And feel the silly tears prick at my eyes.

Fresh

'Your hands are old,' she marvelled. 'Mine are fresh!'
She spread her little paws for him to see
The rosy nails, the tender dimpled flesh
Of a small Miss who'd reached the age of three.
New woolly lambs who cry with plaintive tongue,
Kittens and puppy-dogs and soft-eyed calves
Can melt a heart of stone when they are young –
Nature sees to that – and not by halves.

So what goes wrong? Young children of to-day
Still start off fresh, unspoiled and eager-eyed,
But what of us who should protect and guide?
The untrained shoot reverts back to the wild,
So do the rambling rose, the errant child,
Without restraining hands along the way.

Feelings

'My feelings hurt!' you said, and crossed your arms.
    Crimson-faced you stomped off down the hall
    To sit alone, incensed, beyond recall,
Eyes full of tears. No blandishments or charms

Could win you back. In every inch of you
    Sharp anger crackled. What the hidden cause
    Or how we'd broken your unwritten laws
I'm not quite sure, perhaps we never knew.

How did we heal at last that burning sore?
    I think old Rupert Bear, a trusted friend,
    Edged round the door, pleading that war should end.
You smiled, reluctantly. You were just four!

And so to bed. 'Sleep tight, my love, sleep tight,'
We said, and anger vanished in the night.

Hope

Bright star, never leave me,
    Illumine my days
Though Sorrow bereave me
And Fortune deceive me,
    Snaring my ways.

When chances grow slimmer
    I search for your light,
Though it start to grow dimmer
If it stay but a glimmer
    I know I'm all right.

I can't live without you,
    Oh quickening flame,
Though storms rage about you
And all the world doubt you
    Hope is your name
    Hope is your name.

Night Horrors

I watch the evening star descend,
Taking my joy, my darling love,
While bat-like in the vault above
Death seems to skitter without end,
To mop and mow, not come as friend.

Thank God! At last the star of morn
Returns in radiance and grace,
Night horrors flee that shining face,
In aching heart and soul forlorn
Life quickens as the day is born.

'New hopes for old!' the blackbird cries
'Time to forget the shattered schemes,
The broken bits of battered dreams,
All sullen grief, all wishful lies,
And greet the dawn with glad surmise.'

So let us bury in the past
Dead loves, dead sorrows, dead desires,
The ardent heart to more aspires.
Be resolute, cut free at last,
Who travels light may travel fast.

And when Death's struck and scored with us
Why tremble? We have paid the fare,
And not alone we journey there;
Ten thousand others board with us
That giant celestial omnibus!

The Happy Hour

When Winter's got his hooks in me
And his low days match moods of mine
Then through my thoughts, deliciously,
Curl little tendrils of the vine,
With dream of harvest white or red
From press that crushed and grapes that bled

To make the wine. No Maenad I
Nor yet with topers in cahoots,
But though bleached white in Christian dye
I'm still dark pagan at the roots
And thrill to feel the vinous flood
Coursing warmly through the blood.

Soon, black as waters of the Styx,
Night will engulf my little day.
Roll on, oh Happy Hour of six
When boys and girls come out to play!
I cook the evening meal with verve
If Dionysus steels my nerve.

Thank God for wine that makes us glad
And blunts the edges of disaster.
The pagan god's a likely lad,
Good servant but a rotten master.
His power's not easy to withstand
If once he gets the upper hand.

'Wer spricht von Siegen?'

After Rilke

Who talks of winning? Winning through's my aim
Under such chancy stars. I can't deny
I'd like to hit the jackpot, all the same.
The golden prize has always passed me by.

We cannot choose at birth how we are made
Or what the sort of hand we should be dealt.
Fate is a joker who is not afraid
To hit us poor dumb fools below the belt.

What use to knuckle under in despair?
A bonny fighter though his cause be wrong
Will snap his fingers at the storm-dark air
And meet disaster with defiant song.

Some though let hiccups set them back a mile
And that's what keeps them in the rank and file.

Percy Horton.

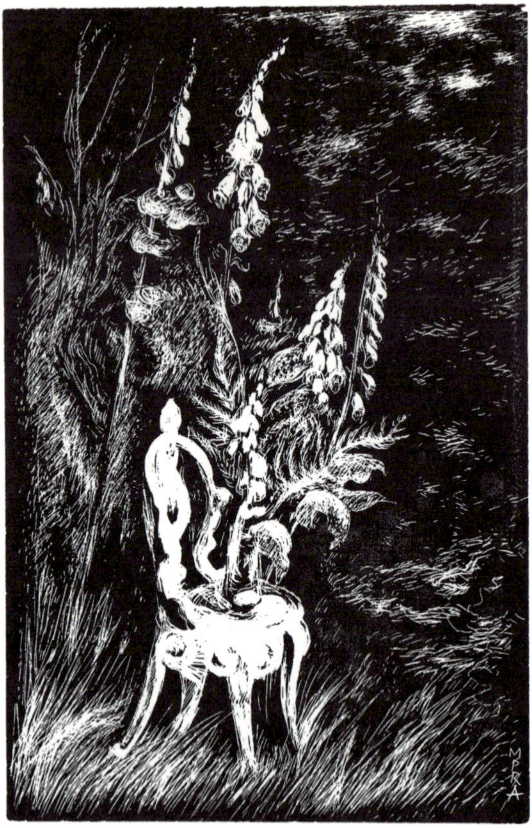
MPRA

Rendezvous

Your chair still stands here halfway up the path
towards the terrace where the roses bloom
on the south wall; deserted, like your room,
your chair's now part of death's sad aftermath.

Here silence speaks, more eloquent than words;
here now the foxglove drooping in distress,
leans on the chairback in a half-caress
till twilight stills the calling of the birds

and halts the booming of the bumble bee
who loves to raid those rosy freckled flowers
and hum away the sleepy noontime hours
in concert with the far sound of the sea.

Here you would rest on the laborious trip
that brought you to the garden's upper reach
whence you might view the sea, the curving beach
and the white sail of some small sailing ship.

'How near he seems!' you said and caught your breath
and smiled as one who goes to meet her love,
serenely trusting in a God above
and that reunion promised after death.

Massed Choirs in Westminster Abbey, 1937

These soaring arches and these dim grey walls
Are but the fair material counterpart
Of a more still and secret sanctuary,
A shrine unseen within this outward shrine,
Ringed round with singing most austerely sweet
And music mounting to the vaulted roof,
Its echoes falling in a wall of sound,
Within whose bounds the questing soul released
Seeks deeper knowledge of its hidden self,
Entrenchéd so against the outer world.

How fair they are, those mighty walls of song!
Builded of such melodious masonry
Of interwoven cadences, the deep
Men's voices and the soaring notes of boys.
Of Faith they sing, of Charity and Hope,
And how a man, though he had all things else,
Had less than nothing, having none of these;
For Faith has steadfast eyes fixed on the stars,
And Hope goes crowned with flowers that wither not,
But Charity transcendeth even these,
For it is loving-kindness manifest,
It is deep understanding from the heart,
It is that spark of Godhead in a man
Fanned into flame to warm a beggared world.

Going Home

Are things chance or are they meant?
Solve me the riddle if you can.
God's ways are not the ways of man.
I can't translate His testament.

Yet I believe. In what? In whom?
The force of good, the power of prayer,
A Being who is always there
At peaks of joy or pits of gloom.

I believe, therefore I hope.
I cannot say I comprehend,
Nor am too certain of my end
As through uncertainties I grope

But know, though far the spirit roam,
Love, whence it came, must call it home.

Fairy Godmother

Of course the Prince was charming. Yes, but where
Would Cinderella be, I ask myself,
Without her fairy godmother to care?
Why, almost certainly upon the shelf,
Hauling the coals, shoeless, her feet in blisters,
Dancing attendance on those ghastly sisters!

Cinders

'Give us a fag', she said, 'lend us a light,
You've got street cred, you look like you're alright.
Once I was fit like you, these days I'm raw.
Times ain't as easy as they was before.

But when I'm out of it in clouds of smoke
It's like I sees again this lovely bloke.
He stopped and checked me out one summer's day.
He looked real good, he did. He was ok.

He took me dancing. When I lost me shoe
"Spark up!" says he, "I really fancy you!"
He took me home, and when he'd paid the score,
"So long!" says he, but never come no more ...

Give us a fag, me dear, lend us a light.
You've got his smile. I knows you are alright.'

Early Words

'Gone away!'
How soon we learn
The small sad words
That grieve and burn

'Gone away!'
I wonder when
The one that's gone
Will come again

Maybe in the spring
Maybe in the fall
Maybe, Christ have mercy,
Never at all.

The Silver Pig

Amongst your things I found a silver pig,
Poised neat as ninepence on a silver box
Containing matches, bijou, not too big,
A pretty pig, a charming paradox.

Au revoir was etched around the base
Love Dick and then the date told all
1916. I wonder, did your face
Light up to see it? Did the quick tears fall?

Was he your love before the other one?
(The married one who could not leave his wife?)
Dick who? Dick dead, his course still left to run?
And did you settle then for half a life?

That war to end all wars was long ago;
Now you're dead too and I shall never know.

Small Survivor

The rape was brutal, scorching, searing pain
And no remission. Again and yet again
The shrinking body quivered in the dust
As all the soldiers gratified their lust
Then left the girl for dead. The nightmare scene
Was now a travesty of what had been
A prosperous village full of peaceful folk.
All fled, or dead, in shroud of evil smoke.

At last came night, with night the will to live
For hunger is a strong imperative.
She did not die. Half-crazed by many ills
She made her way in secret through the hills
To reach a distant hamlet spared from war
Where cousins lived, where she had lived before
In happier days. Up that familiar street
Starving she crawled, collapsing at their feet.

How did she do it? God alone can tell.
One in a thousand could survive such hell.
In time she bore a babe, swore he should die,
But when she saw the tiny creature lie
Helpless and crying, alien, yet her own,
She found her bitter hatred almost gone.
She put the small survivor to her breast,
Half-drowned in tears, and Nature did the rest.

First Born

My thoughts like dark reminders fall
On my small son sleeping curled,
That he does not belong to me at all
He belongs to himself and the world.

He who was fashioned with so much care
From my flesh and blood and bone
Must climb up life's uncertain stair
To death's dark door alone.

Carry a child beneath your heart,
Fear for his welfare early and late
But know that his life is a thing apart,
Already the world is at the gate.

What I thought was mine is not mine at all.
This wonder, this treasure is hard to hold.
Already the unknown voices call
And my darling is only a few days old!

Plus ça Change

The bad old gods, the mad old gods
Have all gone down the drain,
Or so we hear. Myself I fear
They've all come back again.

The dreaded Bs that move in threes
Beëlzebub and Baal
And Belial, he who's vile to see
As djudjus in the kraal.

Moloch as well who's straight from hell
And burns kids for his pleasure
And Mammon, cold, obsessed by gold
And greedy for more treasure.

Do not despair: what's bright and fair
Deserves a headline banner.
The tabloid press cheers up life's mess
With latter-day Diana.

In days of old a huntress bold
Receiving adoration.
She's now returned, fresh plaudits earned,
The idol of a nation.

To a china john

Oh you poor downtrodden john!
Forever being sat upon
Seems a rather unkind fate,
Although you are inanimate.

How lucky that you can't attack
Your oppressors and bite back.
If such a thing should come to pass
It might disturb our gravitas.

Silver Jubilee 1977

Dear Rose of England, Scotland's Queen,
And Wales with all her valleys green,
    Queen of Ulster and the Isles,
Defender of the Faith, no less,
We love you for your steadfastness,
    Your kindly talk, your brilliant smiles.

Lionheart and flower-face,
ELIZABETH, by God's good grace
    For five years and a score,
Although those shoulders seemed too slight
To bear a burden far from light
    You graced it more and more.

Sovereign lady of our time,
In Commonwealth of every clime
    Belovéd you have been.
The gentle girl, the radiant bride,
Serene with *PHILIP* by your side,
    Long live the Queen!

Rosaceous

For Fernand and Helga

I never knew until today
The apple and the rose were kin,
Kissing cousins you might say
Relatives beneath the skin.
So too the Arab and the Jew,
Poised on Armageddon's brink,
Had more in common than they knew
And closer ties than one might think.

All things relate. Pulled straight or thrawn
The threads weave out their secret way,
Mysterious as mushroom spawn
And hidden from the light of day.
To whose design the plan is drawn
A wiser one than I must say.

Poh Lin

When small Poh Lin was rising ten
The illness struck; one dreadful night
She lost her hearing and her sight.
Nor would she ever see again,
Nor hear, poor child. What terror then,
Black terror, filled her empty days.
Touch alone informed her ways.
Like some poor creature in its den.

She raged, became the little prey
Of violent moods, knew the extremes
Of tortured hopes, nightmarish dreams,
And grew more troubled day by day.
Then a blind teacher came her way,
Who knew what means must be deployed
To make the breakthrough, bridge the void,
Bring colour to her world of grey.

Blind taught the blind. With patient skill
He found ways to communicate,
Break down the wall, unlock the gate
Of that shut mind and prisoned will.
He persevered long months until
He taught her braille. She learned to type
Gained a degree when time was ripe,
For all that was a blind girl still.

Year of the Goat is Chan Poh Lin
Funny, wilful, poor but strong
Butting her lonely way along
Playing a hand that's hard to win
Grudging the years' remorseless spin.
'This once-wild girl is fifty soon,
And what *is* Life?' she wrote last June.

Richer with friends like you, Poh Lin!

The French Children

They have sent me their picture, les enfants de Vergnes
Charles and Matthieu and the little girl Laure,
Matthieu's in a cart, Charles makes the wheels turn
And Laure's all dressed up, a toddler no more.

The garden's so quiet now the children have gone
No 'Bonjour, Madame' to cheer up the day.
Whom now shall I practise my rusty French on?
Or buy cassettes for? Or watch as they play?

New children have come, but it is not the same
Though why this should be I am not quite sure.
But there's no carry-on, and life seems quite tame
Without Charles and Matthieu and the little girl Laure.

And how big they have grown! It's easy to see
They will soon have forgotten both London and me.

Low Days

What is this grey miasma, this chill mist,
This nothingness, this feeling of despair,
This dreadful deadweight of the leaden air,
This dark denial that will yet persist?
Death in the mind, the enemy within,
Numbness of heartstrings too inert to feel,
Dullness of eye, clamp on the feathered heel,
Annihilating every effort to begin
Once more, to face and stem the evil tide
That drowns the spirit in a sea of mud
And clogs the ardent courses of the blood.
For what remains when once the will has died
And all our little world is turned awry?
Nothing, a weary yawn, a hopeless sigh.

Giddy Nights

Round and round the pendant light
underneath the ceiling
the bats pursue their endless flight
circling without keeling
with wing-beats rhythmical and slow,
regardless of the guests below.

Tonight upon the midnight hour
the great moon lily bears its bloom,
pulsating into fragrant flower
and scenting all the drawing-room.
It flowers but once in a decade
and that's why all this fuss is made.

Tonight Lucinda seeks her love,
delectable in low-cut dress,
oblivious of the bats above,
driven by some strong duress,
crazed by the magic of the East,
and sadly caring not the least

for husband, children, family ties,
or what the folks back home might say.
She only has impassioned eyes
for dashing Reggie Holliday
and all her heart begins to sing
with hopes of what the night may bring.

The night brings madness; and desire,
when slaked, betrays its sordid side.
Love's flame becomes a sputtering fire
when the avenging Furies ride.
Lucinda breaks her marriage vows
and gets a black eye from her spouse.

The Prudent Gardener

'Ungrateful rose, so full of hate!
How can you prick the hand that feeds?
You have thorns that lacerate,
See how my poor finger bleeds!
What's the use of being smart
If you are not kind at heart?'

'My beauty is a loaded gift,'
Replied the rose with icy scorn,
'If I'm to give the world a lift
I need each sharp and pointed thorn
To keep myself inviolate
From Philistines who desecrate.
Some would blight and some would maim,
Beauty is not understood,
Nor virtue either, more's the shame,
Life is harshest for the good.
I am made as I am made.
Approach me. Do not be afraid.'

But as he wanted to survive
He left her in her lonely state,
Man needs some honey for his hive
When he is searching for a mate.
He scrutinised the garden bed
And settled on heart's-ease instead.

Apples of Gold

'A word fitly spoken is like apples of gold in pictures of silver.'
Proverbs XXV 2

Like apples of gold are words fitly spoken,
rimmed in bright silver they hang on the bough;
grant me such words before the bowl's broken
and the last cord is loosed – oh, grant me them now!

This is a longing more urgent than passion,
a drive more compelling, a trust to fulfil,
a late-flowering love, though a bit out of fashion,
I have cherished it always – I am true to it still.

I would weave my poor lines in a web of such wonder
that all would be caught and all comprehend.
Fool that I am, for that I could plunder
time, sleep and health until my life's end.

The thoughts of the heart and the work of the hands
only one can inspire. Only one understands.

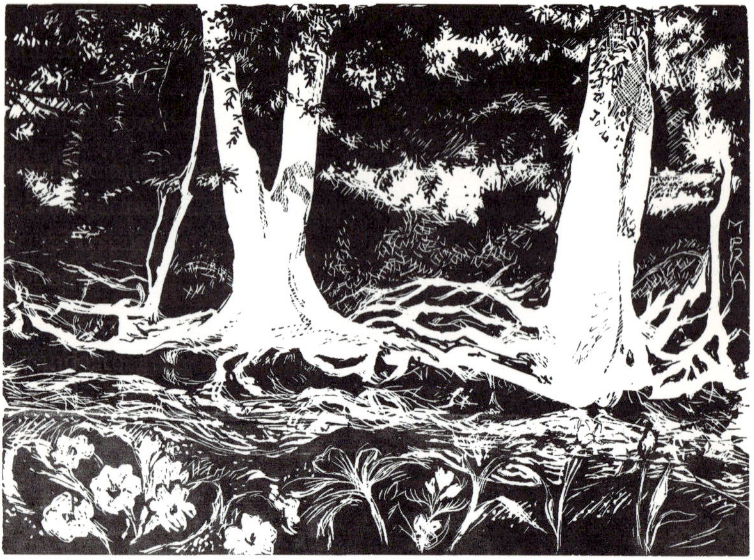
MPRA

Little Werrar Wood

In Werrar Wood the primrose grows
Near as splendid as the rose,
Big as florins, thick as cream,
By tangled root and winding stream.

Here too, where copse and cornfield merge
Are rare bee orchis, bugloss, spurge,
And purple eye of violet
Blinking at a badger's sett.

Last night I dreamt of Werrar Wood
And felt its magic in my blood.
There is a mystery and a grace
All about that little place.

What happened there? I do not know.
Stupid me, to puzzle so.
I only know that God is good
At Eastertime in Werrar Wood.

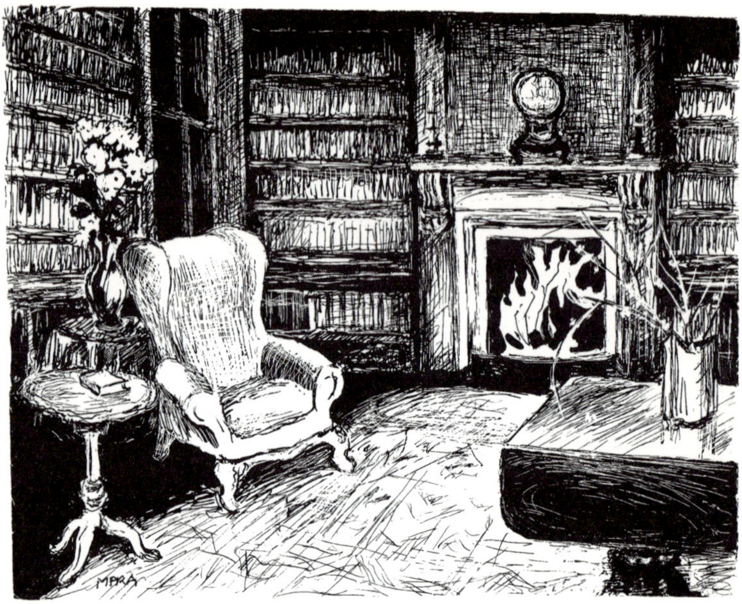

December Legacy

Leave me your books; like you the year is dying.
The jasmine flowers, but I am desolate.
Black dawns, black days and sorrow at the gate,
Eyes all puffed up and red from too much crying.

Leave me your books, my loneliness forestalling,
So brave they stand like soldiers on their mark
To chase the paper tigers of the dark
And see off Death himself if he comes calling.

Leave me your books; you'll live between their covers
Now and for ever. What is time indeed?
You will be always with me as I read.
Leave me your books, last legacy of lovers

So I may find, as grief plays out his part,
The winter jasmine flowering in my heart.

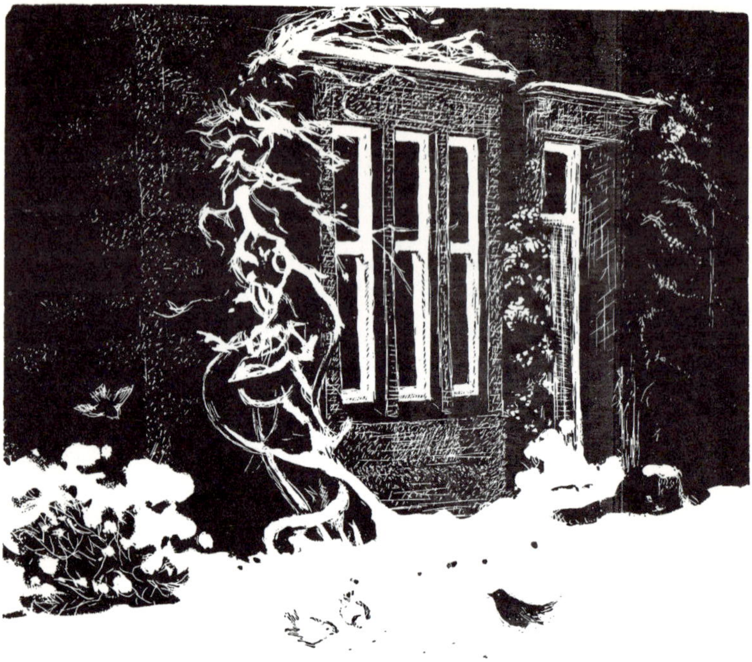

Foursquare

For Mary Allan

Your friendship like your house still stands foursquare
To all the winds that blow;
When I return I know I'll find you there
The same as long ago.
The years between will all dissolve in air
Light as the falling snow;
Your friendship like your house will stand foursquare
To all the winds that blow.

Illustrations

The illustrations facing pages 15, 25, 37, 41, 61, 63 and 65 are by Mary P.R. Allan.

Mary Allan is a graduate of Glasgow School of Art. She has exhibited at the Royal Scottish Academy and the Glasgow Art Institute, and her work is to be found in private collections and the Glasgow Art Gallery.

The illustration facing page 17 is by Nigel Greenhill.

The photograph facing page 19 of Granny-in-Scotland (Deborah McCulloch, 1856–1945) is from a family album.

The line drawing facing page 21 shows Alice St. George being proposed to by Horace Stedall. The artist George du Maurier (1834–1896) was a friend of the Stedall family.

The pen and chalk portrait of Angela Greenhill facing page 38 was made in 1945 by Percy Horton RA.

Notes

Page 17   *Thyme in Sabratha*. Robin, our gifted and much loved second son, became ill in his twenties and died in 1986.

Page 33   *Feelings*. This poem was included in the recent anthology 'The West in Her Eye', edited by Rachel Lever.

Page 49   *First Born*. Shortly before the battle of El Alamein, when the situation in Egypt was uncertain, I travelled by ship to South Africa to have our first child, Nigel, while my husband remained with the Army in Cairo.

Page 53   *Rosaceous*. The line in the poem which also is the title of this collection was suggested to me by the following passage by Fernand Auberjonois: ' Ce que je veux dire, c'est que tout se tient, rien n'est jamais sans rapport avec autre chose.' From ' La Réponse au Grand Large'.

Page 54   *Poh Lin*. Elizabeth Choy, the distinguished former Director of the School for the Blind in Singapore, has provided me with further details of Chan Poh Lin's remarkable career. Granted a scholarship to Perkins School for the Deaf and Blind in Watertown, Mass., U.S.A. by its Director, Dr. Waterhouse, she studied for 11 years before returning to Singapore to teach typing and arts and crafts to blind children.

Page 57   *Giddy Heights*. The names and the incident are all fictitious. No reference is intended to any living or dead person.

Page 65   *Foursquare*. Mary Allan and I were at school together in Scotland. It has been an unusual and special experience to resume a friendship through the making of this book.